God's Little Instruction Book on Love

HONOR
BOOKS

Tulsa, Oklahoma

God's Little Instruction Book on Love
ISBN 1-56292-0723
Copyright © 1996 by Honor Books, Inc.
Published by Honor Books
P.O. Box 55388
Tulsa, Oklahoma 74155

9th Printing

Introduction

Love. It's the most celebrated and beloved theme among men and women alike. It is also the least understood subject in the history of mankind! From season to season, people of all ages seek to find love in the different relationships of their lives. Between spouses it is called *amour* — love captivating a man and a woman. Between friends it is called *phileo* — love bringing trust and security. And between God and man it is called *agape* — love which is infinite and unconditional. In this pocket-size little book, all of these celebrated love themes intertwine.

Feast on heartfelt and impassioned quotes from around the world, bolstered by truths from Scripture. You will delight in how these short yet mighty tidbits of wisdom will illuminate your spirit, stimulate your thoughts, and warm your heart!

Delight your family members and friends with the gift of *God's Little Instruction Book on Love.* It's the book for everyone who ever loved or hoped to love!

L ove is a great beautifier.

And I want women to get in there with the men in humility before God, not primping before a mirror or chasing the latest fashions but doing something beautiful for God and becoming beautiful doing it.
1 Timothy 2:9-10
The Message

But I say unto you, Love your enemies, bless them that curse you, do good to them that hate you, and pray for them which despitefully use you, and persecute you.
Matthew 5:44 KJV

∾ ∾ ∾

Those who deserve love the least need it the most.

6

Love is an act of will, both an intention and an action.

*Let us not love
with words
or tongue
but with actions
and in truth.
1 John 3:18*

∾ ∾ ∾

Each one of you also must love his wife as he loves himself, and the wife must respect her husband.
Ephesians 5:33

∾ ∾ ∾

There is no more lovely, friendly, and charming relationship, communion, or company than a good marriage.

Whoso loves believes the impossible.

[Love] always protects.
1 Corinthians 13:7

∾ ∾ ∾

[Love] is not self-seeking.
1 Corinthians 13:5

∾ ∾ ∾

A good marriage is that in which each appoints the other guardian of his solitude.

L ove must be
the foundation,
the cornerstone.

*If I give all I
possess to the
poor...but
have not
love, I gain
nothing.
1 Corinthians
13:3*

∾ ∾ ∾

Whoso findeth a wife findeth a good thing.
Proverbs 18:22
KJV

∽ ∽ ∽

My most brilliant achievement was the ability to persuade my wife to marry me.

12

We did not guess that love would prove so hard a master.

My command is this: Love each other as I have loved you.
John 15:12

∾ ∾ ∾

[Love] rejoices with the truth.
1 Corinthians 13:6

∾ ∾ ∾

Things and people are not what we wish them to be or what they seem to be. They are what they are.

American women expect to find in their husbands a perfection that English women only hope to find in their butlers.

Be completely humble and gentle; be patient, bearing with one another in love.
Ephesians 4:2

∾ ∾ ∾

Your love has given me great joy and encouragement.
Philemon 7

Presence strengthens love.

16

Absence sharpens love.

I long to see you, so that I may be filled with joy.
2 Timothy 1:4

Live happily with the woman you love through the fleeting days of your life.
Ecclesiastes 9:9
TLB

∾ ∾ ∾

You have a lifetime to enjoy one another. Don't waste a day of it.

Love is hundreds of tiny threads which sew people together through the years.

Be kind and compassionate to one another, forgiving each other, just as in Christ God forgave you. Ephesians 4:32

∾ ∾ ∾

Love is kind.
1 Corinthians
13:4

∾ ∾ ∾

Even the God of Calvin never judged anyone as harshly as married couples judge each other.

No man or woman really knows what perfect love is until they have been married a quarter of a century.

Love is patient.
1 Corinthians
13:4

[Love] endures everything [without weakening].
1 Corinthians 13:7 AMP

∾ ∾ ∾

It was an unspoken pleasure, that having come together so many years, we had endured.

Only choose in love a woman whom you would choose as a friend if she were a man.

Prisca and Aquila, my fellow workers in Christ Jesus,...risked their lives — endangering their very necks — for my life.
Romans 16:3-4
AMP

∾ ∾ ∾

For three years I never stopped warning each of you night and day with tears. Now I commit you to God.
Acts 20:31-32

∾ ∾ ∾

Love is what you've been through with somebody.

24

With each new discovery, love becomes more precious.

And this is my prayer: that your love may abound more and more in knowledge and depth of insight.
Philippians 1:9

How much better is thy love than wine! and the smell of thine ointments than all spices!
Song of Solomon
4:10 *KJV*

∾ ∾ ∾

Physical union with a wife is a source of friendship, a sharing together in a great mystery.

Talk not of wasted affection. Affection never was wasted.

I will very gladly spend for you everything I have and expend myself as well.
2 Corinthians 12:15

Let my beloved come into his garden, and eat his pleasant fruits.
Song of Solomon 4:16 KJV

∾ ∾ ∾

You can keep your love alive if you give it priority in your system of values.

Be to his virtues very kind. Be to his faults a little blind.

He is altogether lovely. This is my beloved, and this is my friend.
Song of Solomon 5:16 KJV

29

Let love and faithfulness never leave you; bind them around your neck, write them on the tablet of your heart.
Proverbs 3:3

∾   ∾   ∾

You are a team. You are not working independently but for one another.

How do I love thee? Let me count the ways.

The Lord said to me, "Go, show your love to your wife again."
Hosea 3:1

∽ ∽ ∽

*How fair you are,
my love, he said,
how very fair.
Song of Solomon
4:1 AMP*

∾ ∾ ∾

Pillow talk between partners can soften a rocky pilgrimage.

Resolve that which can be settled, and negotiate that which is open to compromise.

Do not merely look out for your own personal interests, but also for the interests of others.
Philippians 2:4
NASB

*And we know
that God causes
all things to
work together
for good to those
who love God.
Romans 8:28 NASB*

∾ ∾ ∾

Love is always in the mood of believing in miracles.

L ove is the active concern for the life and growth of that which we love.

Do not withhold good from those who deserve it, when it is in your power to act.
Proverbs 3:27

∾ ∾ ∾

This is how we know that we love the children of God: by loving God and carrying out his commands.
1 John 5:2

∾ ∾ ∾

We can never know completely what we do not love.

We can only love what we know.

I thank my God every time I remember you. Philippians 1:3

Come to me,
all you who are
weary and
burdened,
and I will give
you rest.
Matthew 11:28

ᔕ ᔕ ᔕ

L ove makes everything
that is heavy light.

L ove carries a burden
which is no burden.

For my yoke is easy, and my burden is light.
Matthew 11:30

Let our lives lovingly express truth in all things — speaking truly, dealing truly, living truly.
Ephesians 4:15
AMP

∾ ∾ ∾

This is what marriage really means: helping one another to reach the full status of being persons, responsible beings who do not run away from life.

Love gives naught but itself and takes naught but from itself.

For God so loved the world, that he gave his only begotten Son.
John 3:16 KJV

∾ ∾ ∾

A wife of noble character who can find? She is worth far more than rubies. Her husband has full confidence in her.
Proverbs 31:10-11

∾ ∾ ∾

Being the right person is as important as finding the right person.

Passion should be occasional and common sense continual.

Be clear minded and self-controlled.
1 Peter 4:7

∽ ∽ ∽

*Live by the Spirit,
and you will
not gratify
the desires of the
sinful nature.
Galatians 5:16*

∾ ∾ ∾

Learn to wait and assess instead of reacting from untrained instinct.

Love possesses not nor would be possessed.

*Love does not delight in evil.
1 Corinthians 13:6*

Love never fails
— never fades
out or becomes
obsolete or
comes to an end.
*1 Corinthians
13:8* AMP

∾ ∾ ∾

If thou must love me, let it be for nought except for love's sake only.

Immature love says: "I love you because I need you." Mature love says: "I need you because I love you."

This is how we know what love is: Jesus Christ laid down his life for us. And we ought to lay down our lives for our brothers.
1 John 3:16

∽ ∽ ∽

Be gentle and ready to forgive; never hold grudges.
Colossians 3:13
TLB

∾ ∾ ∾

A good husband should be deaf and a good wife should be blind.

He who is in love sees newly every time he looks at the object beloved.

Like a lily among thorns is my darling among the maidens.
Song of Solomon 2:2

∾ ∾ ∾

For the despairing man there should be kindness from his friend.
Job 6:14 NASB

∿ ∿ ∿

There are deep sorrows and killing cares in life, but the encouragement and love of friends were given us to make all difficulties bearable.

L ove is everything it's cracked up to be. It really is worth fighting for, being brave for, risking everything for.

How great is the love the Father has lavished on us!
1 John 3:1

∽ ∽ ∽

None can tell what to make of it: 'Tis not money, fortune, raving, stabbing, hanging, romancing, swearing, desiring, fighting, dying, though all those have been, are, and still will be mistaken and miscalled for it.

The acts of the sinful nature are obvious....But the fruit of the Spirit is love.
Galatians 5:19,22

〜 〜 〜

'Tis very much like light, a thing everybody knows.

God is light.
1 John 1:5

∾ ∾ ∾

It is for freedom that Christ has set us free. Stand firm, then, and do not let yourselves be burdened again by a yoke of slavery.
Galatians 5:1

∾ ∾ ∾

If love...means that one person absorbs the other, then no real relationship exists any more.

L ove, the quest.

The entire law is summed up in a single command: "Love your neighbor as yourself."
Galatians 5:14

∾ ∾ ∾

You...were called to be free. But do not use your freedom to indulge the sinful nature; rather serve one another in love.
Galatians 5:13

∾ ∾ ∾

Marriage, the conquest.

Divorce, the inquest.

If you keep on biting and devouring each other, watch out or you will be destroyed by each other.
Galatians 5:15

∾ ∾ ∾

All the believers were together and had everything in common. Selling their possessions and goods, they gave to anyone as he had need.
Acts 2:44-45

∾ ∾ ∾

Love does not consist in gazing at each other but in looking together in the same direction.

Familiar acts are beautiful through love.

If the willingness is there, the gift is acceptable.
2 Corinthians 8:12

Though he was rich, yet for your sakes he became poor, so that you through his poverty might become rich.

2 Corinthians 8:9

∾ ∾ ∾

I try to give to the poor people for love what the rich could get for money.

L ove strives toward more than it attains.

Forgetting what is behind and straining toward what is ahead, I press on toward the goal. Philippians 3:13-14

∾ ∾ ∾

"Lord, how often shall...I forgive?" Jesus said to him, "Up to seventy times seven." Matthew 18:21-22 NASB

∾ ∾ ∾

Love is an act of endless forgiveness, a tender look which becomes a habit.

The advantage of love at first sight is that it delays a second sight.

But God demonstrates his own love for us in this: While we were still sinners, Christ died for us.
Romans 5:8

∾ ∾ ∾

Don't be afraid;
just believe.
Luke 8:50

∾ ∾ ∾

Love argues not of
impossibility.

There are few people who are not ashamed of their love affairs when the infatuation is over.

Flee from sexual immorality. All other sins a man commits are outside his body, but he who sins sexually sins against his own body.
1 Corinthians 6:18

Greater love has no one than this, than to lay down one's life for his friends.
John 15:13 NKJV

∾ ∾ ∾

If we would build on a sure foundation in friendship, we must love our friends for their sakes rather than for our own.

Deceive not thyself by over-expecting happiness in the married estate.

Continue to show deep love for each other, for love makes up for many of your faults.
1 Peter 4:8 TLB

∾ ∾ ∾

Yet I hold this against you: You have forsaken your first love.
Revelation 2:4

∾ ∾ ∾

The magic of first love is our ignorance that it can ever end.

We can recognize the dawn and the decline of love by the uneasiness we feel when alone together.

God did not give us a spirit of timidity, but a spirit of power, of love and of self-discipline.
2 Timothy 1:7

Each of us should please his neighbor for his good, to build him up.
Romans 15:2

∾ ∾ ∾

If I truly love another, I will obviously order my behavior in such a way as to contribute the utmost to his or her spiritual growth.

Love fulfils and accomplishes much, where one not a lover falls and lies helpless.

Pity the man who falls and has no one to help him up! Ecclesiastes 4:10

*In a little while
you will see me
no more, and
then after
a little while you
will see me.*
John 16:16

∾ ∾ ∾

No one worth possessing
can be quite possessed.

There isn't a particle of you that I don't know, remember, and want.

I went to sleep, but my heart stayed awake. I dreamed that I heard the voice of my beloved.
Song of Solomon 5:2 AMP

∾ ∾ ∾

If ever a man and his wife absolutely lay aside all good breeding,...their intimacy will soon degenerate into a coarse familiarity, infallibly productive of contempt or disgust.

[Love] does not act unbecomingly.
1 Corinthians
13:5 NASB

∽ ∽ ∽

Love is the only passion which includes in its dreams the happiness of someone else.

Do not let your hearts be troubled. Trust in God; trust also in me. I will come back and take you to be with me that you also may be where I am.
John 14:1-3

I consider my life worth nothing to me, if only I may finish the race and complete the task the Lord Jesus has given me.
Acts 20:24

∾ ∾ ∾

I want relations...based upon some unanimous accord in truth or belief, and a harmony of purpose.

The formula for achieving a successful relationship: treat all disasters as if they were trivialities but never treat a triviality as if it were a disaster.

Let your gentleness be evident to all.
Philippians 4:5

∽ ∽ ∽

Give, and it will be given to you. A good measure, pressed down, shaken together and running over, will be poured into your lap. For with the measure you use, it will be measured to you.
Luke 6:38

∾ ∾ ∾

Love is the one business in which it pays to be an absolute spendthrift: Give it away; throw it away; splash it over; empty your pockets; shake the basket; and tomorrow you'll have more than ever.

Love, like a lamp, needs to be fed out of the oil of another's heart, or its flame burns low.

Do not let any unwholesome talk come out of your mouths, but only what is helpful for building others up according to their needs, that it may benefit those who listen.
Ephesians 4:29

∽ ∽ ∽

[The adulteress] gives no thought to the way of life; her paths are crooked, but she knows it not.
Proverbs 5:6

∾ ∾ ∾

One can find women who have never had one love affair, but it is rare to find any who have had only one.

It is only when we no longer compulsively need someone that we can have a real relationship with them.

May you rejoice in the wife of your youth. Be captivated by her love.
Proverbs 5:18-19

∾ ∾ ∾

Come, my lover, let us go to the countryside, let us spend the night in the villages....
There I will give you my love.
Song of Songs 7:11-12

∾ ∾ ∾

Each coming together of man and wife...should be a fresh adventure.

Each winning should necessitate a fresh wooing.

All beautiful you are, my darling; there is no flaw in you.
Song of Solomon 4:7

～ ～ ～

If the king regards me with favor and if it pleases the king to grant my petition and fulfill my request...
Esther 5:7-8

∾ ∾ ∾

It's a woman's privilege to change his mind.

Seeing eye to eye in marriage often requires the bigger person to bend a bit.

The king asked Esther, "Now what is your petition? It will be given you."
Esther 5:6

∾ ∾ ∾

God made mankind upright, but men have gone in search of many schemes.
Ecclesiastes 7:29

∾ ∾ ∾

There is no way to take the danger out of human relationships.

"Beware you be not swallowed up in books! An ounce of love is worth a pound of knowledge."

Knowledge puffs up, but love builds up.
1 Corinthians 8:1

∾ ∾ ∾

Like Sarah...You are her daughters if you...do not give way to fear.
1 Peter 3:6

∾ ∾ ∾

Love is being willing to face risks to see your spouse's dreams come true.

Too much love never spoils children.

Let the little children come to me, and don't prevent them... And he put his hands on their heads and blessed them.
Matthew 19:14-15
TLB

∾ ∾ ∾

Bear one another's burdens, and so fulfil the law of Christ.
Galatians 6:2 RSV

∾ ∾ ∾

Sharing the housework makes it easier to share the love.

In so far as one denies what is, one is possessed by what is not.

Saul [jealously] eyed David from that day forward.
1 Samuel 18:9
AMP

∽ ∽ ∽

Do not say, "I'll pay you back for this wrong!"
Proverbs 20:22

∾ ∾ ∾

Incompatibility: the taste for domination.

You can give without loving, but you cannot love without giving.

Excel in this grace of giving. I am not commanding you, but I want to test the sincerity of your love.
2 Corinthians 8:7-8

Many waters cannot quench love; rivers cannot wash it away.
Song of Solomon 8:7

∾ ∾ ∾

It is a fact that other people, even people who love you, will not necessarily agree with your ideas, understand you, or share your enthusiasms.

L ove believes that it may and can do all things.

The only thing that counts is faith expressing itself through love.
Galatians 5:6

A wife of noble character is clothed with strength and dignity; she can laugh at the days to come.
Proverbs 31:10,25

∽ ∽ ∽

Married life requires shared mystery even when all the facts are known.

Marriage: it's an agreement for the mutual forgiveness of sin.

Love each other deeply, because love covers over a multitude of sins.
1 Peter 4:8

∾ ∾ ∾

My command is this: Love each other as I have loved you.
John 15:12

*L*ove, and do what you like.

To love anyone is nothing else than to wish that person good.

Nobody should seek his own good, but the good of others.
1 Corinthians 10:24

∾ ∾ ∾

Woman is not independent of man, nor is man independent of woman.
1 Corinthians 11:11

∾ ∾ ∾

Good battle is healthy and constructive, and brings to a marriage the principle of equal partnership.

Every year the aches get a little stronger, but the ache for my sweetheart grows deeper.

My soul yearns for you in the night; in the morning my spirit longs for you.
Isaiah 26:9

∾ ∾ ∾

You who are simple, gain prudence; you who are foolish, gain understanding.
Proverbs 8:5

∾ ∾ ∾

A bride at her second marriage does not wear a veil. She wants to see what she is getting.

God's grace is the oil that fills the lamp of love.

It is God Who is all the while effectually at work in you — energizing and creating in you the power and desire — both to will and to work for His good pleasure.
Philippians 2:13
AMP

≈ ≈ ≈

Where the Spirit of the Lord is, there is freedom.
2 Corinthians 3:17

ove rules without a sword. Love binds without a cord.

Love makes all hard hearts gentle.

The mind controlled by the Spirit is life and peace.
Romans 8:6

Be kind and compassionate to one another.
Ephesians 4:32

∾ ∾ ∾

A successful marriage is an edifice that must be rebuilt every day.

He who forgives first, wins.

...forgiving each other, just as in Christ God forgave you.
Ephesians 4:32

Blessed is he whose transgressions are forgiven.
Psalm 32:1

∾ ∾ ∾

My state of bliss is by no means perfect.

You can't make me unhappy.

There is now no condemnation for those who are in Christ Jesus, because through Christ Jesus the law of the Spirit of life set me free.
Romans 8:1-2

Do not worry about how you will defend yourselves or what you will say, for the Holy Spirit will teach you at that time what you should say.
Luke 12:11-12

∾ ∾ ∾

Love can hope where reason would despair.

110

The best friend is likely to acquire the best wife, because a good marriage is based on the talent for friendship.

Let each of you esteem and look upon and be concerned for not [merely] his own interests, but also each for the interests of others.
Philippians 2:4
AMP

∾ ∾ ∾

Marriage is the operation by which a woman's vanity and a man's egotism are extracted without an anesthetic.

Love is not... touchy.
1 Corinthians 13:5 TLB

∾ ∾ ∾

After marriage, a woman's sight [can become] so keen that she can see right through her husband without looking at him — and a man's [sight can become] so dull that he can look right through his wife without seeing her.

What therefore God hath joined together, let not man put asunder.
Matthew 19:6 KJV

∾ ∾ ∾

Love...is not irritable.
1 Corinthians 13:5 TLB
∾ ∾ ∾

To marry means to halve one's rights and to double one's duties.

The marriage state...is the completest image of Heaven and Hell we are capable of receiving in this life.

If you love someone you will be loyal to him no matter what the cost.
I Corinthians 13:7 TLB

∽ ∽ ∽

Can two walk together, except they be agreed?
Amos 3:3 KJV

∽ ∽ ∽

Chains do not hold a marriage together.

116

I have great hopes that we shall love each other all our lives as much as if we had never married at all.

Let us not love [merely] in theory or in speech but in deed and in truth — in practice and in sincerity.
1 John 3:18 AMP

∾ ∾ ∾

Let her be as the loving hind and pleasant doe... always be transported with delight in her love.
Proverbs 5:19
AMP

Any marriage...is infinitely more interesting than any romance, however passionate.

It is the one who is not really in love who says the more tender things.

With persuasive words she led him astray; she seduced him with her smooth talk.
Proverbs 7:21

I consider that our present sufferings are not worth comparing with the glory that will be revealed in us.
Romans 8:18

∾ ∾ ∾

A successful marriage demands a divorce: a divorce from self-love.

We often speak of love when we really should be speaking of the drive to dominate or to master.

All at once he followed her like an ox going to the slaughter, ...little knowing it will cost him his life.
Proverbs 7:22-23

*Do not rebuke
a mocker or
he will hate
you. Instruct a
wise man and he
will be wiser still.
Proverbs 9:8,9*

∾ ∾ ∾

Reason and love keep little company together now-a-days.

Nothing can match the treasure of common memories, of trials endured together.

To Timothy, my dear son. I thank God...as night and day I constantly remember you in my prayers.
2 Timothy 1:2-3

∾ ∾ ∾

Be patient with each other, making allowance for each other's faults because of your love.
Ephesians 4:2 TLB

∾ ∾ ∾

There is love of course. And then there's life....

The fate of love is that it always seems too little or too much.

Confess your faults to one another, and pray one for another.
James 5:16 KJV

Is anyone of you in trouble? He should pray.
James 5:13

∾ ∾ ∾

Have a heart that never hardens, and a temper that never tires, and a touch that never hurts.

Real love...is very rare because most people are strategists.

If I...can fathom all mysteries and all knowledge, ...but have not love, I am nothing.
1 Corinthians 13:2

∾ ∾ ∾

Learn as you go along what pleases the Lord.
Ephesians 5:10
TLB

∾ ∾ ∾

Love is the child of freedom, never that of domination.

L ove is the only force capable of transforming an enemy into a friend.

Don't have anything to do with foolish and stupid arguments, because you know they produce quarrels.
2 Timothy 2:23

∾ ∾ ∾

Through love you should serve one another.
Galations 5:13
AMP

☙ ☙ ☙

Do whatever arouses you most to love.

A husband without faults is a dangerous observer.

Husbands, love your wives, as Christ also loved the church and gave himself for her.
Ephesians 5:25

∾ ∾ ∾

Oh, feed me with your love...
for I am utterly lovesick.
Song of Solomon
2:5 TLB

∽ ∾ ∽

To be able to *say* how much love is to love but little.

What will matter to you at the end of life will be the loving relationships you built....

Be glad for all God is planning for you.
Romans 12:12
TLB

I want men everywhere to lift up holy hands in prayer.
1 Timothy 2:8

∽ ∽ ∽

A good husband and father is really praying all the time.

Marriage: to strengthen each other in all sorrow; to minister to each other in all pain; to be one with each other in silent, unspeakable moments.

Store [up treasures] in heaven where they will never lose their value.
Matthew 6:20 TLB

∾ ∾ ∾

*Live one day
at a time.
Matthew 6:34 TLB*

∾ ∾ ∾

Old patterns will persist if serious effort is not made to change them.

A man must pursue his wife's mind as well as her body.

Let love be your greatest aim.
1 Corinthians
14:1 TLB

∾ ∾ ∾

*Do for others
what you want
them to do
for you.
Matthew 7:12 TLB*

∾ ∾ ∾

Human love...must use the body in the service of the partner's spiritual welfare.

When I have learned to love God better than my earthly dearest, I shall love my earthly dearest better than I do now.

For since a man and his wife are now one, a man is really doing himself a favor and loving himself when he loves his wife!
Ephesians 5:28
TLB

∾ ∾ ∾

Let no debt remain outstanding, except the continuing debt to love one another.
Romans 13:8

∾ ∾ ∾

He who has been victorious in his home can never be completely defeated.

Marriage is a venture into intimacy, and intimacy is opening of one self to another.

Let love be genuine.
Romans 12:9
RSV

∾ ∾ ∾

Make every effort to keep the unity of the Spirit through the bond of peace.
Ephesians 4:3

∽ ∽ ∽

The goal in marriage is not to think alike but to think together.

There is no winning or losing in a good conflict, but a breaking through to better understanding of each other.

Love does no wrong to anyone. It is the only law you need.
Romans 13:10
TLB

∽ ∽ ∽

Love one another deeply, from the heart.
1 Peter 1:22

∾ ∾ ∾

A successful marriage requires falling in love many times, always with the same person.

L ove is too young
to know what
conscience is.

*Rid yourselves
of all malice and
all deceit. Like
newborn babies,
crave pure
spiritual milk, so
that by it you
may grow up.
1 Peter 2:1-2*

∾ ∾ ∾

How you capture my heart. Look the other way, for your eyes have overcome me!
Song of Solomon 6:4-5 TLB

∾ ∾ ∾

Love is the strange bewilderment which overtakes one person on account of another person.

There is no remedy for love but to love more.

Live a life of love.
Ephesians 5:2

*Take delight
in honoring
each other.
Romans 12:10
TLB*

∽ ∽ ∽

Keep thy eyes wide open before marriage, and half shut afterwards.

Love thrives in the face of all life's hazards, save one — neglect.

Each one of you also must love his wife as he loves himself, and the wife must respect her husband. Ephesians 5:33

149

The fruit of the Spirit is... patience.
Galatians 5: 22

∾ ∾ ∾

It takes patience to appreciate domestic bliss.

Knit your hearts with an unslipping knot.

Marriage should be honored by all, and the marriage bed kept pure.
Hebrews 13:4

We're not two...
competing
individuals.

*Be quick to listen,
slow to speak
and slow to
become angry.
James 1:19*

∿ ∿ ∿

152

We dare not to try to make it on our own.

Remember that you and your wife are partners in receiving God's blessings.
1 Peter 3:7 TLB

Do not repay evil with evil or insult with insult, but with blessing, because to this you were called so that you may inherit a blessing.
1 Peter 3:9

∾ ∾ ∾

Love is often a fruit of marriage.

"I love you." It means: "You, you, you. You alone."

Live considerately with [your wives],...in order that your prayers may not be hindered and cut off. — Otherwise you cannot pray effectively.
1 Peter 3:7 AMP

∾ ∾ ∾

Whoever would love life and see good days must ...seek peace and pursue it.
1 Peter 3:10-11

∾ ∾ ∾

Love is growing up.

References

Acknowledgements

Louisa May Alcott (5), M. Scott Peck (7,70), Martin Luther (8), Elizabeth Barrett Browning (9,31,46), Rainer Maria Rilke (10), Bette Davis (11), Winston Churchill (12), Robert Bridges (13), Epictetus (14,44,94), W. Somerset Maugham (15), Thomas Fuller (16,17,67), Dr. James Dobson (18,28,33,133,136,137,153), Simone Signoret (19,116), Wilfrid Sheed (20), Mark Twain (21), Lillian Hellman (22), Joseph Joubert (23), James Thurber (24,146), Plutarch (26), William Wadsworth Longfellow (27), Janette Oke (30), Muriel James (32), J.C. Powys (34), Erich Fromm (35,47), Thomas Ã` Kempis (38,39,61,64,71,95), Paul Tournier (40), Khalil Gibran (41,45), Robertson Davies (43), Ralph Waldo Emerson (49), John Oliver Hobbs (50), Erica Jong (51), The Ladies Dictionary, "Love" (52,53), Ann Oakley (54), Helen Rowland (55,56,102,112,113), Antoine de Saint-Exupéry (58,123), Percy Bysshe Shelley (59), Mother Teresa (60), Peter Ustinov (62), Natalie Clifford Barney (63), Francois, Duc de La Rouchefoucauld (65,80), Charlotte Bronte (66), Benjamin Disraeli (68), Jean de La Bruy'ere (69), Sara Teasdale (72), Noél Coward (73), Lord Chesterfield (74), Karr (75), D.H. Lawrence (76,108), Quentin Crisp (77), Beecher (79), Anthony Storr (81), Marie Carmichael Stopes (82,83), H.W. Platt (84), Collie (85), Barbara G. Harrison (86), John Wesley (87), Paul Lewis (89), Ursula K. Le Guin (91), Ambrose

Bierce (92), Amy Carmichael (93), Richard Ford (96), Henrik Ibsen (97), Augustine (98), Aquinas (99), Ann Landers (100), H.W. Beecher (103), Herbert (105), Andre' Maurios (106), William Penn (107), Irving Layton (109), Lyttelton (110), Friedrich Nietzsche (111), Arthur Schopenhauer (114), Sir Richard Steele (115), Lord Byron (117), W.H. Auden (118), Marcel Proust (119), P. Frost (120), Thomas Szasz (121), William Shakespeare (122,145,151), Jean Anouilh (124), Amelia Barr (125), Charles Dickens (126), Anita Brookner (127), Erich Fromm (128), Martin Luther King (129), St. Teresa (130), Lord Halifax (131), Petrarch (132), V. McNabb (134), George Eliot (135), H. Gibert (138), C.S. Lewis (139), Robert W. Burns (140), David Augsburger (141), R.C. Dodds (142), Carole Mayhall (143), Mignon McLaughlin (144), H.D. Thoreau (147), Benjamin Franklin (148), John Dryden (149), Santayana (150), Mrs. Norman Vincent Peale (152), Moliere (154), Walter Trobisch (155), J. Baldwin (156).

Additional Copies of this book and other titles in the
God's Little Instruction Book series are available at your local bookstore.

God's Little Instruction Book
God's Little Instruction Book II
God's Little Instruction Book for Mom
God's Little Instruction Book for Dad
God's Little Instruction Book for Graduates
God's Little Instruction Book for Students
God's Little Instruction Book for Kids
God's Little Instruction Book for Couples
God's Little Instruction Book for Men
God's Little Instruction Book — Special Gift Edition
God's Little Instruction Book Daily Calendar
God's Little Instruction Book for Women

Tulsa, Oklahoma